Problem Solving with Pigs

By R. Mann Harasymiw

GS
MATH

Please visit our website, www.garethstevens.com. For a free color catalog of all our high-quality books, call toll free 1-800-542-2595 or fax 1-877-542-2596.

Library of Congress Cataloging-in-Publication Data

Harasymiw, R. Mann.
Problem solving with pigs / by R. Mann Harasymiw.
  p. cm. — (Animal math)
Includes index.
ISBN 978-1-4339-9324-4 (pbk.)
ISBN 978-1-4339-9325-1 (6-pack)
ISBN 978-1-4339-9323-7 (library binding)
1. Problem solving—Juvenile literature. 2. Mathematics—Juvenile literature. 3. Swine—Juvenile literature.
I. Title.
QA63.H37 2014
513—dc23

First Edition

Published in 2014 by
Gareth Stevens Publishing
111 East 14th Street, Suite 349
New York, NY 10003

Designer: Nicholas Domiano
Editor: Therese M. Shea

Photo credits: Photo credits: Cover, p. 1 TaXZi/Shutterstock.com; pp. 3–24 (background texture) Natutik/Shutterstock.com; pp. 5, Ulrich Mueller/Shutterstock.com; p. 7 Petar Paunchev/Shutterstock.com; p. 9 Ammit Jack/Shutterstock.com; pp. 11, 13, 15, 19 iStockphoto/Thinkstock.com; p. 17 Mircea BEZERGHEANU/Shutterstock.com; p. 21 Eduard Kyslynskyy/Shutterstock.com.

Printed in the United States of America

CPSIA compliance information: Batch #CS13GS: For further information contact Gareth Stevens, New York, New York at 1-800-542-2595.

Contents

Boldface words appear in the glossary.

Oink!

Many farms raise pigs. Did you know pigs are smart? They can help us **solve** math problems! Check your answers on page 22.

A farmer has 4 pigs. She gives 2 pigs to a friend. How many pigs does the farmer have left?

Many Names, Many Colors

Pigs, swine, and hogs are all the same animal. Boy pigs are called boars. Girl pigs are called sows.

A farmer has 2 boars and 10 sows. How many pigs does the farmer have in all?

Pigs can be many colors. White pigs look pink. Others are black, brown, and even reddish! Some pigs have spots, too.

Six pigs are in the barn. Half of the pigs have spots. How many pigs have spots?

Snouts

Pigs can't see well, but they can smell food from far away! A pig's nose is called a snout.

A farmer needs 7 pigs. He has 2 pigs. How many more pigs does the farmer need?

Pigs on farms eat a lot of corn. Some pigs use their snouts to dig for food.

There are 5 pigs in the barn. Three pigs take a nap. The others go outside. How many pigs go outside?

Piglets

Baby pigs are called piglets.
They're tiny at first. They grow fast.
Adult pigs are very heavy!

A sow has 6 piglets. Another sow has 3 piglets. How many piglets are there in all?

Dirty but Cool

Pigs roll around in mud to stay cool. However, they like to be clean.

The Green Farm has 4 pigs. The Blue Farm has 5 pigs. The Red Farm has 2 pigs. Which farm has the most pigs? Which has the fewest?

17

Pigs on Tiptoe

Pigs have 4 toes on each of their 4 feet. Each toe ends in a **hoof**. The pig walks on just 2 toes of each foot. It tiptoes!

How many toes does a pig have on 2 feet? How many toes are on all 4 feet?

Wild Pigs

There are wild pigs, too! Wild pigs have straight tails. Farm pigs have curly tails.

Three pigs are on the farm. Two wild pigs are in the woods. How many more pigs are on the farm than in the woods?

21

Glossary

hoof: the hard covering on the feet of some animals

solve: to find the answer

Answer Key

page 4: 2 pigs

page 6: 12 pigs

page 8: 3 pigs

page 10: 5 pigs

page 12: 2 pigs

page 14: 9 piglets

page 16: Blue Farm, Red Farm

page 18: 8 toes, 16 toes

page 20: 1 more pig

For More Information

Books

Macken, JoAnn Early. *Pigs*. Pleasantville, NY: Weekly Reader Publishing, 2010.

Searl, Duncan. *Pigs*. New York, NY: Bearport Publishing, 2006.

Sexton, Colleen. *Piglets*. Minneapolis, MN: Bellwether Media, 2008.

Websites

Animal Bytes: Wild Swine

www.sandiegozoo.org/animalbytes/t-wild_swine.html
Read about the kinds of pigs that live in the wild.

Pigs

kids.nationalgeographic.com/kids/animals/creaturefeature/pigs/
See photos of pigs and read more about them.

Publisher's note to educators and parents: Our editors have carefully reviewed these websites to ensure that they are suitable for students. Many websites change frequently, however, and we cannot guarantee that a site's future contents will continue to meet our high standards of quality and educational value. Be advised that students should be closely supervised whenever they access the Internet.

Index